ONCE UPON A
PARABLE

Illustrationed by Hilber Nelson

MACK THOMAS

Gold 'n' Honey BOOKS

GOLD 'N' HONEY FAMILY CLASSICS

To D.R.G.
Sower, Seeker, Storyteller

ONCE UPON A PARABLE

published by Gold'n'Honey Books
a part of the Questar publishing family

© 1995 by Questar Publishers, Inc.
Illustrations © 1995 by Hilber Nelson
Designed by David Uttley

International Standard Book Number: 0-88070-746-1

Printed in Mexico

Scripture quotations are from *The Greatest Story,* © 1994 by Western Seminary

For information:
Questar Publishers, Inc., Post Office Box 1720
Sisters, Oregon 97759

95 96 97 98 99 00 01 02 — 10 9 8 7 6 5 4 3 2 1

Behind Jesus was the Sea of Galilee.

In front of Him was a sea of faces — so many people pressing in so close,

that Jesus had to step into an idle fishing boat

and push out from shore.

He seated Himself in the boat, as it rocked lazily in the gentle waves.

The sun beating down was hot. But a breeze blew off the sea.

It cooled His back, and it cooled all the faces that were turned to see Him.

Around the boat, sun sparkles danced on the water.

Then Jesus opened His mouth to speak. And with His words

He painted pictures.

As people listened and sometimes closed their eyes from the sun's glare,

they could see in their minds the pictures Jesus painted,

and think about them — which is what Jesus wanted them to do.

Some saw very little in the pictures.

But others — even young children — saw much more.

Hearing Jesus' words, some people could see as high as heaven.

Some could see as far away as the end of time.

A special few could see as deeply as the bottom of their own hearts.

And how about you? What do *you* see in the pictures Jesus painted?

FROM MATTHEW 13:1-3

A Sower

MATTHEW 13:3-23

IG JIM FREELEY reached again into the seed pouch hanging at his waist. Out came his hand, filled with more seed than most people could hold in their hat. Big Jim's hands were huge.

With all but two fingers open, his hand slung to the right. Wheat seed scattered across the bare dirt in that direction. Then the last two fingers flew open as his hand jerked to the left. Just as much seed scattered that way. He scooped into the seed pouch for the next handful, and took a step forward.

Here on the slopes of Bearpaw Ridge, Big Jim was helping his neighbor, Isaac Bonney, to plant his fields. Big Jim did this every spring. He loved to help his neighbors. And he loved to work hard — the harder the work, the bigger his smile.

But today, Big Jim Freeley wasn't smiling. His mind was on the boys' class at Bearpaw Valley Church which he had taught every Sunday for sixteen years.

"Maybe it's time I quit," he was telling himself.

As he scattered another handful of seed, he looked uphill. Mr. Bonney and a team of oxen were breaking ground, getting it ready for the seed. The field was empty and lifeless. Mr. Bonney's face looked lifeless too. His head drooped forward.

Earlier this morning, Big Jim heard bad news from this old farmer — more bad news about Billy, his runaway son. Billy Bonney, it seemed, had been in a terrible fight. He had shot a man. Now the law wanted to find Billy and throw him in jail.

Suddenly Jim wiped his eyes with the back of his big hands. He thought he'd seen young Billy on that tree swing up the hill. But no — it was just a memory. Billy would never be a boy again. He might never be home again either.

"Where do you think he is?" Big Jim had asked Isaac as they were walking to the barn at sunrise.

"Don't expect I'll ever know," Mr. Bonney quietly answered. "Maybe out west b'now."

"He's so young," Big Jim said sadly.

"Yeah. So young," Mr. Bonney replied, his voice a little shaky. "But so hard. And so mean."

Big Jim shook his head, and laid his hand on Mr. Bonney's shoulder.

Not many years ago, Billy was in the boys' class at church. Big Jim couldn't remember a single Sunday when Billy wasn't a troublemaker. He either laughed at the other boys or threatened to hurt them. If Big Jim asked a question, Billy would ignore it, or maybe say something sour. Still, Big Jim tried to love him.

One day Billy seemed interested for the first time in the lesson. Big Jim had just men-

tioned how Jesus raised Lazarus from the dead. This was new information to Billy.

"How could he do that?" he had asked. It was the first question Big Jim had ever heard from him.

"Nothing's impossible with God," the teacher answered, looking straight into Billy's wide-open eyes. "Not a thing."

Billy lifted his head and considered this new thought.

"Nothing," Big Jim said again, with firmness.

Suddenly Billy's eyes narrowed, his head lowered, and he snickered. "I'm impossible," he said. He shook his fist and yelled at the other boys: *"I'm impossible! I'm impossible!"* Big Jim finally got him quiet, but by then class time was over.

Jim shook his head at the memory of Billy's yelling that day. It was as if someone reached into the boy's head and snatched away the words of God he had just begun to hear. It was so discouraging to a teacher. Jim could feel the discouragement, like chains around his neck.

"I'm impossible," he said. He shook his fist and yelled at the other boys: "I'm impossible!"

Lord, Big Jim prayed silently, *what's the use in me teaching that class? I can't change those boys...*

The seed pouch was empty. Big Jim walked to where a seed barrel stood at the edge of the field. As he filled his pouch from the barrel, he glanced at the path leading to the cabin. Blackbirds were stealing stray seed that had fallen there.

He remembered at once the Bible parable he was teaching the boys next Sunday, now that planting time was here. He repeated it in his mind:

> *A farmer went out to sow his seed. Some seed fell on the pathway where it was trampled, and birds swooped down and ate it.*
>
> *Other seed fell on rocky places, where there was little soil. It quickly sprouted up. But because it had no root, it withered as soon as the sun rose to scorch it.*
>
> *Other seed fell into a thorn patch where thorns choked out any growth.*
>
> *But some seed fell on good soil and produced a crop...*

Big Jim's thoughts were interrupted by a shout behind him: *"Howdy there! Need another hand?"*

Turning, he saw someone riding tall on a horse. It was Adam Andrews.

Jim gave a big wave. He hadn't seen Adam in a coon's age. Adam had been in his class the same time as Billy. He was older now, and living and working on a farm over in High Point Valley.

Adam couldn't stop talking as he drew near and dismounted. "When I rode into town," he said, "and heard you were up here working, I just had to come help. Besides, you've got to hear about the new boys' class I'm teaching at High Point Church. I'm awful glad you showed me how — Sunday after Sunday, always giving us restless boys the good Word! Maybe you didn't think it was sinking in. But you'd be amazed how often I remember things you told us.

"Yep, you're the kind of teacher every boy needs. Say, you're keeping at it, aren't you? You'll never stop teaching, will you?"

Big Jim had to smile. He picked up a handful of seed from the barrel and let it slowly sift through his huge fingers.

"I suppose I'd better not," he said. He reached for Adam's wrist, and let some seed drop into the young man's hand. "I reckon we should both keep at it," Jim told him.

He looked out across the plowed, empty ground — the good, rich soil. It was easy now to imagine how it would look this fall, covered with golden grain.

Good Fish

MATTHEW 13:47-50

ANO RAN through the jungle. When he stepped into the clearing by the sea, he gave a little groan. The men had already dragged the giant net to shore. Everyone was at work with the catch. They would wonder where he had been.

Kano slipped quietly to where men were sorting the fish. Every fish was picked up and looked at. Every good fish went into a basket for food. All the others — all the bad fish that did not taste good — were thrown away.

"Kano!"

His grandfather, walking up from the boats, had seen him.

"Yes, Grandpapa?"

"Kano, where have you been?"

"At the banana grove."

Kano didn't say he had been playing there with his monkey, Pobo.

"We needed you here working," his grandfather said, frowning at the boy.

"Papa sent me for bananas," Kano said.

He didn't mention that it was yesterday when his father had sent him.

His grandfather looked hard at him. "Be a good fish, Kano. Find someone to help you carry one of these baskets to the spring."

Kano found his friend Tanoa down by the boats. The two boys got on either side of a big basket filled with fish. They carried it along a path through the jungle to a freshwater spring, where the fish would be cleaned. Kano's father was at the spring, kneeling with other men beside the water. He had a fish in one hand and a bone-knife in the other.

"Kano," he said, "I asked you to help with the catch this morning. Where have you been?"

"At the banana grove," the boy answered. He knew his father would want a fuller explanation. "Mama sent me for bananas," he added. The boys set the heavy basket down.

"Kano," his father said, looking hard at his son. "Your mother's at the fire-pit. Be a good fish, and take these to her." He pointed to a smaller basket of fish that were cleaned and ready to roast.

Carrying the smaller basket, Kano took a path that went a little further in the jungle. It led to a clearing with a large roasting pit in the center. His mother and other women were there. To roast the fish, they were wrapping them in banana leaves and palm fronds.

"Kano," she said when she saw him, "we need more banana leaves. Please go and get some. And bring bananas, too."

Kano set the basket of cleaned fish beside her.

"Kano?" she said quietly.

"Yes, Mama?"

"You missed the catch this morning. And the work. Where were you?"

"At the banana grove," he answered.

She said nothing, waiting for more.

He did not want to lie. But he could think of nothing else. "Grandpapa sent me for bananas," he finally said.

His mother looked hard at him. "Bring us the leaves now," she said. "Be a good fish."

Kano stepped along the path that went deeper through the jungle.

In the banana grove, he found his monkey again. "Help me, Pobo. Help me gather leaves." The monkey only screeched at him.

Kano crossed his arms. "What are you saying, Pobo? Are you saying I'm not a good fish? Are you saying I'm really a bad fish? Because I don't tell the truth?"

Pobo screeched again.

Kano picked up a stick. Into the jungle, he threw it as hard as he could. He felt tears in his eyes. "Well," he said to Pobo, "maybe you are right."

Late in the day, all the families of the island came together in the clearing by the fire-pit. The feast was almost ready.

Kano was in a curving palm tree at the edge of the clearing. He had spent most of the afternoon there. He didn't feel like talking with anyone.

Kano was staring at the fire-pit, where the coals still glowed red. They were so hot that no one got close. In his mind Kano pictured how awful it would be to fall into the pit.

> *Kano picked up a stick. Into the jungle, he threw it as hard as he could. He felt tears in his eyes. "Well," he said to Pobo, "maybe you are right."*

He saw his grandfather hold up his hands. Everyone in the crowd became quiet. He heard Grandpapa's prayer of thanksgiving for the big catch. Then he watched him open the island's only Bible, and read aloud these words:

The kingdom of heaven is like a dragnet thrown into the sea, where it caught all kinds of fish.

When it was filled and hauled up on shore, workers sat down and sorted all the good fish into baskets. The bad fish they threw away.

Grandpapa looked around at the people's faces. Then he kept reading, and Kano kept listening.

That is what it will be like at the end of this age. The angels will go out and remove the wicked from the godly, and throw them into the fire. In that awful place there will be weeping and gnashing of teeth.

Then Kano's grandfather began praying once more. But now Kano didn't hear the words. He hurried down from the tree. His eyes were nearly blinded by tears. Finally he found his mother and father. He reached out his arms, and buried his face in his father's side. "I don't want to be a bad fish," he cried. "I don't want to be thrown in the fire!"

His parents bent over him. "Kano, what is it?" his mother asked.

"I keep lying!" Kano blurted. "I don't want to!"

He could say no more. He could only cry.

Grandpapa came closer, and Kano heard his father tell him what Kano had said.

Grandpapa kneeled before the boy, and laid his Bible on the ground between them. He took Kano's hands in his.

"Kano, we are all bad fish," Grandpapa said, "until Someone makes us good. Do you want to hear how that happens?"

Kano sniffed, and nodded.

Grandpapa smiled. "Then let me tell you the Story," he said.

A Vineyard

MARK 12:1-9

ALVADOR LIFTED to his shoulders the huge basket filled with grapes. He heaved it up the same way he saw his uncle do it, but staggered for a moment under the weight. Then he regained his balance, and followed in his uncle's footsteps.

Down between the long vine-rows they walked, their feet pressing hard on the sandy soil. Salvador's face and hair were soaked in sweat.

He heard a quick breeze rustling across the vineyard. He wanted to set down the basket and stretch his arms, and enjoy the wind on his face. But he kept going, step after heavy step behind Diego. The breeze went away.

Salvador had come to the country to help his uncle. Before sunrise this morning they had walked from his uncle's house to the vineyard. "Show me today how hard you can work," Diego had said. "If you're a good worker, you can stay with us as long as you like. If not, you may have to go back to the city."

Salvador did not want to go back. He had no family in the city now, for his mother and father had died, and he was their only son.

Salvador stayed close to his uncle as they worked, doing everything his uncle did. They were always together, but they said almost nothing. They worked hard.

At the end of the row stood the watchtower and winepress. It was the most beautiful vineyard building Salvador had ever seen. It was as beautiful as a church.

Before its arched entryway, they set down the baskets. Other workers took them inside. Salvador and his uncle picked up empty baskets nearby, for another load.

As they turned to go back, Salvador took a quick glance upward at the tower. "Tio Diego," he said quietly, "why does the watchtower have a cross on top?"

"The owner put it there," his uncle answered, "to help everyone remember what happened here."

"What happened?"

"I must tell you," Diego said, walking quickly through the vine-rows, "but not now. When the workday is over, you can hear the story."

There were many more hours of labor that day. Salvador kept up with his uncle, watching and learning all he did.

Finally the sun lowered, the watchtower bell rang out, and the workday ended. Diego sat on the vineyard wall and said goodbye to other workers leaving for home. Salvador sat beside him, glad to be off his aching feet. Then Diego said quietly, "This is the story:

"The owner of this land is a good man, a patient man. He loves this land, and this vineyard. He carefully planted the vines. He built this wall to keep out pesky animals. He built

the watchtower to look out for thieves and fire. And he put a winepress under the tower, where the grapes could be squeezed.

"He hired workers to care for the vines and work the harvest. He promised them a large share of the fruit.

"Then he had to move away, to care for business in the city. When the first harvest came, he sent a servant to his vineyard to bring him a sample of the fruit. And when the workers heard the servant's request, what did they do? They beat him, and chased him away."

"No!" Salvador cried.

Diego paused. "If you had been the owner, Salvador, what would you do?"

"I would get rid of those workers, and never hire them again."

"So would I," said Diego. "But the owner is a good man, a patient man. He sent another servant. This time the workers threw stones at him and gashed his head. He, too, returned to the owner with no fruit."

Salvador shook his head, hardly believing what he heard.

"The owner sent a third servant," Diego continued. "But they beat and wounded him as well. The owner sent even more servants — yet the workers always attacked them. Some they even killed."

"Surely that was the end of it!" Salvador said. "Surely the owner had those workers thrown in prison forever!"

"No," answered Diego. "It wasn't the end. The owner decided to send his son to the vineyard — his only son, whom he loved above all else. He said, 'Surely those workers will respect my own son!'

He could not bear to hear the story go on like this. He held a fist to his lips.

"The workers recognized the son at once when he rode through the gate. They quickly made a plan. They knew the son would someday own this land after his father, but they wanted the property for themselves. So they decided to destroy him.

"They charged at him and pulled him from his horse, and threw him over the wall. Then they rushed over it themselves and beat him — till he was dead."

Salvador flinched at his uncle's words. He could not bear to hear the story go on like this. He held a fist to his lips.

"And then, Salvador?" he heard his uncle say. "What do you think the owner did next?"

"What else could he do," Salvador said slowly, "but come and destroy those workers?"

"Truly," said Diego, "there was nothing else to do. Then the owner brought in new workers who would respect him and give him fruit at harvest time. These are the workers you labored with today in the owner's vineyard.

"Come, Salvador," Diego said, as he slipped down from the wall.

Salvador followed. "And the cross?" he asked, pointing up. "On the tower?"

"What happened in this vineyard," Diego replied, "is exactly what happened in a story Savior Jesus told about Himself. Perhaps someday you'll forget what happened here. But you must never forget the story Jesus told. Look at that cross, and remember how He was killed by those who should have respected Him, and respected His Father God.

"Salvador, no matter where you go in this world, you are in God's vineyard. He's the owner. The only reason you're here on His land is to give Him the fruit He wants.

"He sent His Son here once — then people killed Him. Soon He'll send Jesus to us again. Let's make sure this time that we have plenty of fruit to give Him.

"Now then," Diego said, "let's go home. Anyone who works as hard as you must be hungry."

Salvador nodded at his uncle's smile. He would work even harder for the owner of this vineyard, now that he knew his story. He followed Diego out the gate, then looked back. The sun's last rays were touching the tower. The cross shone red in the light.

A Tree and Its Fruit

LUKE 13:6-9

FINNEY COULDN'T FIGURE it out. Why did his next-door neighbor cut down that other tree? For an apple tree, it had been a real good climber. Finney had spent some fine hours perched in its top, spying on the neighborhood.

He sat down in the shade of the only apple tree left in Mr. Hunter's back-yard. He set his fishing pole and worm can and his morning catch on the ground beside him. He grabbed a ripe apple from a harvest basket nearby, and leaned back.

"Tell me, Sizzle," he said to the cat sleeping above him on a branch. "Why did Mr. Hunter ax down the only good climbing tree he's got?"

Sizzle took no notice of the question or the questioner. "Lazy, no-account critter," Finney said to her. "You've spent your entire life snoozin'. A body ought to tie a brick to your tail and throw you in the river, for all you're worth."

He heard someone whistling. Mr. Hunter's wife stepped out her back door, carrying her empty wash basket. Not seeing Finney, she walked to the line where the week's laundry was hanging dry, and sat the wicker basket at her feet. With her back to him, she started undoing clothespins, letting socks and towels fall in the basket. All the while she was whistling.

Finney thought it would be fun to startle her. He picked up a worm from the can beside him, aimed carefully for Mrs. Hunter's shoulder, and with an underhand toss landed the worm there with his first try.

To Finney's surprise, Mrs. Hunter simply flicked the worm away with the clothespin in

her hand, and never turned around. "I know you're there, Finney," she said. "Saw you before, out my window." She went right on working, and whistling, too.

Finney leaned back again. The tune she was whistling sounded like a church song. "You're right chirpy today, Miz Hunter," he commented.

"I've got good cause to be happy this fine summer morning," she said. "And I reckon you do, too."

"How do you mean?" From the apple he took a big bite that swelled his cheek.

"I noticed you've been fishing," Mrs. Hunter said. "That means you already finished the Bible lesson your father gave you today. Aren't you happy you learned it so quickly?"

Finney stopped chewing the fruit in his mouth. Before leaving for a day-long trip to Springfield early this morning, his Pa had given him a Bible passage to copy down and memorize. He told Finney to learn it all before doing anything else today. But Finney had written down only one verse when he decided it was fishing time.

He swallowed the bite of apple. "Yes ma'am, I learned it all quick as lightning, and I'm mighty glad."

Mrs. Hunter turned and smiled at him, then went back to work. "Memorizing Scripture," she said, "is good for the mind and good for the soul, I'm sure you agree. Why don't you recite your new passage for me?"

Got to think fast, Finney told himself. "Well, ma'am, it's a powerful good passage, and that's for certain.... It's actually about a tree...." He saw his opportunity at once. "Speaking of such, I was wondering why Mr. Hunter cut down that other apple tree here. Do you happen to know why, Miz Hunter?"

"Ah," she answered with a grin. "It was the apples."

Finney had the grateful feeling that this could turn into an extended conversation. "But you know, ma'am," he said, "I don't rightly recall that tree ever bearing any apples."

"Exactly the point, Finney. Years ago, I planted the tree for one reason only: *apples.* When it grew up and didn't give us any, Mr. Finney pruned and fertilized it, and still it never bore fruit. So now he's chopped it down. It was useless. It was a waste of good ground. By the way, Finney, does all that remind you of anything you've heard or read lately?"

"Well, now," Finney said. He had no idea what she was driving at. "I suppose it just might. But what does it remind you of, Miz Hunter?"

She turned toward him, and grinned again. "Why, of course it reminds me of that Scripture lesson you learned this morning."

Finney smiled back at her, and nodded. "Of course," he said in a small voice. Just then Sizzle jumped down from the tree and landed in his lap. It scared him plenty.

Mrs. Hunter laughed. "Yes, Finney, I spoke with your father over the front fence this morning, as he was leaving. He told me about the passage he gave you. I just learned it myself last week. So, if you don't mind, could you listen to me say it, to see if I've got it right?"

"Oh, please do," Finney allowed, shooing away the cat. "Go right ahead."

She stepped away from the clothesline, and stood close to him. "Luke thirteen, six to nine," she began.

A man had a fig tree planted in his vineyard. He came looking for fruit on it, but found none. Then he said to the caretaker of the vineyard, "Look, for three years I've been coming to get fruit from this fig tree, but have found none. Cut it down! Why should it use up good ground?" But the caretaker replied, "Sir, let the tree grow for another year as well, so I can dig around it and fertilize it. If it bears fruit, fine. But if it doesn't, you can cut it down."

"How did I do?" Mrs. Hunter asked.

"It was right slick, ma'am," Finney answered, "and I'm proud of you."

He gathered his things, and stood. "As you know, ma'am, I've got a fish here to fry, and it must be lunchtime, so I'd best mosey on."

"I understand," Mrs. Hunter said. "But before you go..."
She put her hand on his shoulder.

"Before you go, let me tell you what that story means to me. Just like we plant trees to give us fruit, God has planted us here on this earth to bear fruit as well. We're breathing His air and drinking His water and eating His food, and He has a right to expect fruit from us. And the fruit He wants us to bear includes things like — well, like honesty, and obedience to our parents. Don't you agree?"

Sizzle jumped down from the tree and landed in his lap. It scared him plenty.

Finney felt his face getting hot. "Yes, ma'am." Her words pierced through him like a knife.

"If we don't bear that fruit," she continued, "if we tell lies or disobey our parents, then maybe in God's eyes we're like an apple tree that doesn't bear apples. Don't you agree?"

"Yes, ma'am," Finney said. "I see what you mean."

He had more to tell her, but it was hard getting the words out.

"I lied to you," he finally blurted, "and I disobeyed Pa. I'm sorry."

Mrs. Hunter gave him a handshake. "Thank you, Finney, for telling the truth. You're bearing fruit after all!

"Oh, and Finney — I've got an idea. I'll fry that fish for you, while you go home and finish memorizing your Bible passage. When you've got it down cold, come back and tell it to me, and I'll have your lunch waiting for you."

"Yes, ma'am!" Finney said. He took a deep breath of air — God's air — and ran home to his Bible.

Friends

LUKE 11:5-8

FTER THE THREE~BLOCK WALK through the snow from her apartment house, Mossy stepped up to the bakery door, and stomped her boots. *All I want is warm feet,* she told herself. *No, all I want is to turn around and go home.*

With one arm she held a small suitcase. She raised the other to knock on the bakery door. Then she put her hand back in her pocket. Then she raised it again. *Yes, I simply must,* she decided. *For my friend, I absolutely must.*

She knocked. There was no answer. But at this hour she wasn't surprised. She knocked again, harder.

"Who's there?" came a sleepy voice from above. "Tell me who's there."

Mossy stepped back to see the apartment above the bakery. Helen, the baker's wife, had opened a second-story window.

"Hi, Helen!" Mossy called. She held the suitcase in front of her.

Helen frowned. "Mossy! Where are you going at this hour?"

"Back home soon," Mossy answered. She wore her best smile, as if this were a sunny afternoon in May, not a cold winter's dawn.

"But—" Helen pointed at the suitcase. "What's in there?"

"Oh, it's empty." Mossy lifted it high.

Helen bent her head, as if she were filled with questions but didn't know what to ask first. "Then—why are you carrying it?"

"Wouldn't you call me terribly hard and cruel if they didn't find a good breakfast at my table this morning?"

"To hold bread," Mossy answered cheerfully. "It'll stay dry in here, and the loaves won't be smashed on the way home."

"But Mossy! Mossy dear, it's Sunday. The bakery's closed all day. And we're still in bed! You know we can't sell you anything now."

Mossy laughed. "Oh, I don't want you to *sell* me anything! Anyway, you know I've got no money."

Mossy stopped smiling, and stepped forward. "Helen, a friend of mine from down south just arrived on the early train, and her three children with her. They've ridden all that far just to visit me. And they've had nearly nothing to eat the whole way. Now wouldn't you call me terribly hard and cruel if they didn't find a good breakfast at my table this morning? But I tell you, Helen, my pantry's almost bare, and that's a fact. And I simply must take care of my friend. I absolutely must. So I'm humbly asking you to let me borrow three loaves."

Helen leaned further out the window. "Oh, Mossy—"

"Only three loaves," Mossy pleaded. "Yes, that'll be precious plenty indeed."

Helen began again: "Well, Mossy—"

"And you know I'll be ever grateful!" Mossy added. "Ever grateful!"

Helen shouted, "Mossy, don't say another word! Are we friends, or not? Now don't move a step. I'll be at the door in half a second. We'll fill that suitcase with all it will hold." She closed the window.

Mossy breathed a sigh, and stomped her feet.

Back home a while later, Mossy sat down with her friend and her children. On the table before them were fragrant slices of the baker's best bread, plus bagels and doughnuts.

"Mmm," said Mossy's friend, "shall we say a prayer of thanksgiving?"

"Oh, we must," answered Mossy. "We absolutely must."

Mossy's Bible lay next to her plate, where she always kept it. Before praying, she opened the tattered book and read aloud this story of Jesus:

Suppose you must go to a friend at midnight and say, "My friend, may I borrow three loaves of bread? An acquaintance on a journey has just arrived and I have nothing for him to eat." What kind of friend would answer, "Don't bother me! I've already locked up the house for the night and my children are tucked into bed. I can't get up to give you anything"? I'm telling you that even if he won't get up and offer help for the sake of their friendship, yet because of his friend's bold persistence he'll arise and give him whatever he needs.

A Lost Sheep

LUKE 15:4-7

BEL TOSSED A STONE into the stream below. On the meadow nearby, a few sheep skittered from the tiny splash, then resumed their grazing.

This would be Abel's last night here. Tomorrow he would take his family's flock down the valley. The safe time for pasturing in the mountains was ending. During the dangerous storm season, the sheep would be sheltered at his village.

Abel would enjoy being with family and friends again. But he dreaded having to put up with his neighbor Zack, the tax-collector. He and Zack had been boyhood friends, but now Abel considered him a pain at best. Zack was loud, he was selfish, he was—

Oh, why bother about him now, Abel thought, *and ruin my last evening here?*

Abel hoped he and the sheep would rest well tonight, for an early start tomorrow. The journey was long, and his aging father would expect them in the village well before nightfall. Abel didn't want his father to worry.

Zack, of course, would be expecting him too. He would come quickly for an exact count of Abel's flock—in order to collect all the sooner the tax on each head. Once more Zack would probably say, "Yes, they're only sheep. But we may as well tax the stupid creatures, since I'm told there's nothing more dear to a stupid shepherd's heart."

Abel didn't let Zack's words bother him. He was a shepherd because all his family were shepherds, and Abel was proud of them. His grandfather was one of the Bethlehem shepherds on the night Messiah Jesus was born. And Abel's father had heard Jesus tell the story of a man with a hundred sheep who couldn't bear to lose even one.

"Someday, son," Abel's father had told him long ago, "may that story become your own. And remember: There's a time to be like the sheep in that story, and a time to be like the shepherd."

Abel still wondered what his father meant.

Suddenly a gust of wind tore at Abel's cloak. He glanced up. Dark clouds were edging over the mountains, darker than any he'd ever seen.

Sure-footed and fast, he descended his high overlook. Storm season, it seemed, was coming early this year.

Across the meadow Abel hurried. "Don't you fear, now don't you fear," he sang to the sheep, "for I am always here." His flock gathered to follow him.

On the far side of the meadow, he stopped. He lifted a narrow gate made of poles and branches lashed with vines. It was the gate to the sheepfold he had built around a shallow cave in the mountainside. As a boy he had carried and stacked every stone that formed the fence around the fold. With his own hands he had made this a safe place and a good place for his flock.

The sheep crowded at the gate, wide enough for only one at a time. If any sheep stopped in the gateway, Abel at once would call its name. "Move along, Nabber," he would say, and perhaps gently prod Nabber with his staff. But mostly he was silent. The shepherd was counting his sheep.

Thunder rolled down from the mountaintops. The sheep in the fold shuffled nervously toward the cave at the back, bleating loudly.

Stretching out his staff, Abel encouraged the last few stragglers. "Sixty-six, sixty-seven," he announced, as he finally hustled two more through the gate. Two others nearby were grazing quietly as if they thought the storm was no bother after all. "Sassy!" the shepherd called, "and Dan!" His strong voice—and another blast of thunder—got their attention.

Sixty-eight, sixty-nine. With Dan and Sassy safe inside, Abel's hands worked quickly to close the gate. But his worried eyes looked back, searching across the meadow and into the rocks. His flock numbered seventy. One sheep was missing.

He stood on the stonepile fence and looked out for number seventy. No other sheep was in sight.

Once more the thunder rumbled. A stronger blast of wind came, as did the first rain-drops, big and heavy and cold.

Surely he miscounted. Into the fold he jumped, and started again. *One, two, three, four...* His finger punched the air as he stepped slowly toward the cave, where most of the sheep were huddled. His cloak snapped in the wind. Drops of rain trickled down the sides of his face.

But before he reached thirty, a question flashed in his mind. *Where is Tendra?* Tendra, the smallest ewe, thin-coated and scrawny. Tendra, the silent one, whose bleat Abel had never heard.

"Tendra!" he cried.

The sheep pressed close, their faces toward him. He knew his presence kept them calm, with the wind blowing, and rain clattering on the rocks, and the sky growing dark.

He held his hand above his eyes to keep out the rain, and stared back at them. Tendra's face wasn't there.

She was gone. Tendra was lost. She was out in the storm, and she was no match for it.

He leaped over the fence. "Lord God, help me find her," he prayed.

> *The stormwind came in waves, roaring straight at him. It slapped his face, and clawed at his cloak.*

The stormwind came in waves, roaring straight at him. It slapped his face, and clawed at his cloak. Each blow tried to push, push, push him back. Each blast howled, "No! No! No! Go back, go back..."

Halfway across the soggy meadow, he dropped the staff and peered through the driving rain into the mountains. He cupped his hands around his mouth, and yelled against the wind: "Tendra! Little Tendra!"

He snatched up his staff, and struggled up into the rugged rocks.

When the wind finally lessened, the darkness had fallen. Abel fumbled among rain-slickened rocks, across cracks and crevices and over fast-flooding water streaming every-where.

Fighting on, Abel couldn't help thinking of the shepherd story his father heard from Jesus. He knew the story was really about people, not sheep. *Is this really how God looks for us?* he asked himself.

Much later, the rain finally stopped. But Abel was soaked. His arms and shoulders shivered from the cold. He searched on.

He knew she would make no answer, but he cried out again and again into the night: "Tendra! My little one!" His voice grew hoarse. "Tendra, where are you?"

Abel wondered: Did God feel this way — did God *care* this way — about *everyone?* About *anyone?* Even Zack?

Hour followed hour. Once, as his sore and shaking legs tore through a patch of thorny brambles, he looked up. The sky wasn't as black as before. Dawn was near. Soon he would have to take his flock down the valley, with or without Tendra.

Suddenly his foot snagged, and he tumbled over the edge of a deep dropoff. He crashed hands-first onto rough ground. He felt a piercing ache where his side had slammed into a fallen tree branch.

Painfully he scooted away from the jabbing limb, and lay still. In the faint light he could see blood on both his hands.

He dropped his head on his aching arms. He groaned, closing his eyes. His heart pounded furiously, crying for rest.

But he must get up.

"Tendra," he whispered into the ground. "Tendra, my lost one — I'm coming."

He rested his forehead on the dirt, and slowly extended his aching arms along the ground.

His bleeding hands touched something soft and warm.

He raised his head.

"Tendra!"

She stared at him, silent and still.

Her legs were caught in a jumbled heap of thorns and branches that must have been swept down the mountain in the storm. Painfully he moved closer. He carefully freed her, then scooped her into his arms.

He gathered his cloak about her, and sat down to lean against the side of the dropoff, making her comfortable against his chest. He pressed his face against hers.

"Tendra," he whispered. "Silent little Tendra. We must hurry home today. But your journey won't be hard; no, I'll wear you proudly on my shoulders all the way. That's where you'll be when Father greets us.

"And tonight," he said, as he gently stroked her sore legs, "tonight I'll invite neighbor Zack to join us around our fire at home. I'll hold you in my lap, Tendra, and when he asks how many sheep I have, we'll tell him all about our story."

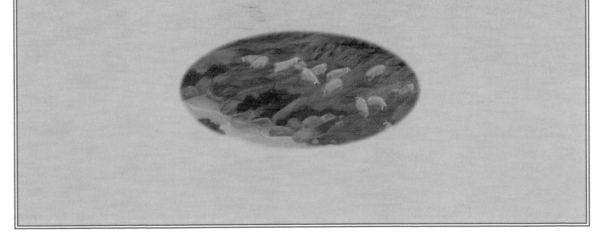

Always Pray

LUKE 18:1-8

ARDLY STOPPING to breathe, Vera poured out her appeal to the judge. She spoke each word carefully, words she had memorized during many sleepless nights.

This was the fourth time she had come before him. Just as before, she did not kneel, nor raise her voice. She was determined to keep her dignity.

"Your honor," she concluded, "our last hope is you. You are the last recourse for a poor woman whose husband has been falsely accused and cast in prison. You are the last refuge for a mother driven from her home with her five children. Your honor, I beg of you: Grant me justice this day!"

Just as before, the judge spoke not a word in answer. With blank eyes, he looked at Vera, and pointed to the door. The scribe nearby coughed, then announced, "You may go."

Struggling to keep her head high, Vera turned, and walked out.

On a hill outside the city half an hour later, she heard her children's muffled voices coming from the cave. As her footsteps sounded on the gravelly slope, she heard one of them whisper, "Shhh!" That, she knew, would be Marcus, her oldest.

In the early evening light, her shadow fell across the cave's entrance.

"I'm back," she said wearily, and stepped inside.

She knew Marcus sensed at once her failed mission. So she said nothing.

She stepped to the back of the cave. The younger children quietly followed. She laid them down in blankets, and kissed each one. Then she sat with Marcus on the ledge at the entrance, where they could watch the dusk fade away. There was nothing else to do. They had eaten their only meal today, and they had no oil to burn in their lamp.

A spark in Marcus's eyes told her he wanted to talk. She wanted to talk with him as well. She waited until she knew the other children were asleep.

"Marcus," she whispered, "The judge will never help us."

She folded her fingers, and placed them to her lips. "I'm afraid for us all," she said. "I'm so tired of trying. And I don't know what to do."

Marcus responded gently: "Mother, while you were gone, we went for a walk. And a woman spoke with us."

Vera's heart flared in fear. "Marcus, no! You dare not speak to strangers!"

"We didn't, Mother," he assured her. "We only listened. She was just a poor woman with pity on some lonely children. And she told us a story from God's book."

The fear left Vera, and the sadness returned. She lowered her head, and rubbed her tired eyes with her fingers. "What story?" she asked.

Marcus seemed glad to tell it. "There was this judge who had no fear of God, and no

respect for people — like our judge. And there was a widow who had been mistreated. She came to ask him for help. Again and again she asked him. Finally, because she kept bothering him, he gave her what she wanted."

Vera studied her son's face in the dying light. How proud his father would be to see him now, and all the children. She was amazed by their boundless hope. Where did it come from? It could not come from her, for she had so little to give. How she hated to say or do anything to quench their fire.

"That widow," she said, "must have been a strong woman. Much stronger than I am."

"I don't know," Marcus answered.

But I know, she told herself. *I know I'm weak, and I know I can't go before that heartless judge again...* She bit her lip to keep from bursting into tears.

"Mother," Marcus continued, "the woman told us more." He was searching for his words. "Mother — Mother, we should pray. Because God is different!"

"What — what do you mean, Marcus?"

"The woman said God isn't like the judge in that story. She said God would *never* refuse to give justice to His people who cry out to him day and night. So we should always pray and not lose heart, because God will give His people justice, and *quickly!* It's right there in God's book."

He stood, reaching out his hand. "Mother, if God is like that, let's pray!"

Slowly she took his hand. She stood beside him, there in the cave entrance. She closed her eyes, then opened them again, and looked out at the evening star. *I'm too weary and weak,* she told herself, *even to pray...*

She heard Marcus's voice as he began: "God... Lord God... we want to know what it's really like to be Your people. Will You help us? We need You. Please, we need You!"

Yes, yes, we need You! In her heart she found the words. She closed her eyes. Soon she was on her knees, weeping and praying.

When they stopped praying long afterward, every star was shining in the black sky. At the cave's entrance, Vera fell into an exhausted sleep.

When she awoke, her first sight was of someone's face gently lit by the earliest morning light. She didn't know who it was, but she felt no fear. She lifted her head.

"Mother," he whispered.

"Marcus!"

"Shhh! Mother, I stayed up watching the stars, and praying to the One who made them." He put his hand on her shoulder. "Mother, we've just spent our last night in the cave. We'll see Father today. I know it!"

She stared at him, amazed that the spark could show in his eyes in such dim light. But the spark told her he was right.

She placed her hand on his. "Then I'll go," she said, hardly knowing where the words came from. "I'll go into the city to the church. I'll pray, until court is in session. Then I'll speak once more to the judge."

She rose and kissed Marcus, then slipped back into the cave's darkness to kiss the others before she left.

Only a few hours later, when she next saw them, her husband was at her side. They had come to the cave to get their children, and take them home.

The Banquet

LUKE 14:16-24

POURING QUICKLY without spilling a drop, Boon Hopper filled the cups of his three customers from a pot of fresh coffee. None of them said thank you.

"Are you sure I can't get you something else?" Boon asked, trying to sound cheerful. They didn't seem to hear him. They kept glancing behind them through the diner's plate-glass windows.

Boon looked at the clock, then started checking and refilling salt and pepper shakers and the sugar dispensers.

"I still can't believe my eyes," one of the customers said, staring outside.

The others — a woman and another man — looked over their shoulders again. Across the street was the arched doorway to a banquet hall. Servants in black suits and ties were greeting people as they arrived. The guests were mostly wearing rags. In fact, it appeared that the servants were collecting homeless people off the streets and bringing them in.

"It's disgusting!" remarked the woman customer. "I thought it might be a costume party. But look at that lady. She's for real! Another of those shabby street people."

Boon looked up from the counter. In the street, a stooped woman in a baggy coat was being helped toward the banquet hall by one of the dapper servants. Boon knew her. She called herself Mary, and she stayed mostly in an alley next to the diner. Boon often gave leftovers from the diner to Mary, and to her homeless friends.

He watched as she tottered up the banquet hall steps. Her face was bathed in golden light that came from inside. *Whatever's happening in there,* Boon told himself, *I hope Mary has a grand time.*

"Looks like a banquet for bums," said the second man at the counter. He sipped his coffee. "I'd be totally humiliated in there. Am I ever glad I declined Johnny's invitation."

"Us too," said the woman. "But it's good we came down to look closer. Now I'm totally convinced we should forget we ever knew Johnny Grace."

The first man shook his head, and stirred his coffee. "Yeah, Johnny's dangerous. I'll never call him a friend again. Though I've known him all my life."

"Religion's what ruined him," the second man added. "The more he got stuck on God, the more I couldn't stand him. Of course I didn't exactly say that to Johnny when he called today, asking if I was coming to his party. I just told him I was going out of town."

"He phoned us too," said the woman. "I told him I felt awful and was staying in bed for a while. But I really would get sick if I had to eat with that trash over there."

Boon looked at the clock again. He'd already kept the diner open an hour longer than usual, just for these three customers. If they planned to stay, he wished they'd order something to eat. He was fiercely hungry himself, but didn't think he should eat in front of customers unless they did too. He stepped closer to the counter.

"Excuse me," he said. "Before I close, couldn't I fix turkey sandwiches for you, or warm up some bean soup?"

The first man turned to him. "What's that? Oh — perhaps later." Then, like the others, he went on ignoring Boon, and looked across the street.

Boys wearing dark jackets and sunglasses were being escorted into the banquet hall.

The second man howled. "Gang members!"

The woman shuddered. "Thank heavens none of our friends showed up. I guess they've all given up on Johnny."

She pulled a cigarette from her purse, and lit it. "You know, it's too bad really," she reflected. "Since we all grew up together, I thought Johnny would sooner or later turn out normal like the rest of us."

They all became silent. In time the scene outside got quiet as well. Boon sorted silver-
ware and folded dishtowels behind the counter. He turned out some lights in back, then
filled his customers' coffee cups again.

"Oh, *no!*" shouted the woman. Boon nearly dropped the coffee pot on the counter.

She pointed across the street, and the others turned to see. "Johnny's come out," She
cried. "He's staring our direction. Look! He's sending someone this way. Maybe he recognized us! He'll try to get us in there! What'll we do?"

The second man stood. "Let's break out of here," he said. "Does this place have a back
door?" he asked Boon.

"Sure," Boon said, and pointed. "This way."

The three customers hurried back with him, then outside into the darkness. Boon
breathed a sigh of relief when he closed the door behind them.

Returning up front, he saw a servant entering the diner. "Mr. Boon Hopper?" he asked.

Boon laid his hands on the counter. "Yeah, that's me."

"Mr. Hopper, you're invited to a twelve-course banquet across the street this evening.
The other guests have been telling our host about you. Mr. Grace wants you to be his guest
of honor at the head table. Can you join us?"

Boon dropped his head and looked doubtfully at his cook's uniform — dirty from the
day's work.

"Oh, and Mr. Grace said you're to come just as you are," added the servant. "Will you?"

Boon smiled. "Why not?" he answered. "I could use a hot meal."

He hopped over the counter, turned out the other lights, and followed the servant out.

Inside the banquet hall, he was ushered to a table in front where a laughing, well-dressed
man introduced himself as Johnny Grace. Mr. Grace stood and thanked all the crowd for
coming, and read aloud this story that Jesus told:

*A man was preparing a large banquet and sent out many invitations. When the date arrived he sent
his servant to tell the guests, "It's time to come. Everything is ready." But all of them together began
making excuses. The first said to him, "I just bought a field, and I must go see it. Please, send my
regrets." Another said, "I just bought five yoke of oxen, and I'm leaving to try them out. Please
excuse me." Yet another said, "I just got married, so I can't come."*

*When the servant reported back to his master, the master angrily told his servant, "Quickly! Go
out into the streets and alleys of the city and bring in the poor, the crippled, the lame, and the blind."
The servant replied, "Sir, we've already done what you commanded, but there's still room." The master said to the servant, "Then go out to the highways and the outskirts of town and compel them to come
in, so my house will be full! But believe me, not one of the guests who were first invited will taste a
single morsel of my banquet!"*

A Lost Son

LUKE 15:11-32

O NE LAST TIME, Sir Perry called out: "Erric, my son, even now you can change your mind. You know I want you to stay!"

But Erric didn't hear. Or if he did, he pretended not to.

Sir Perry watched his younger son ride away with all the boy owned, all that was his share of the family wealth.

This is what Erric said he wanted: to take what was his, and be gone, and be free.

Sir Perry stood at the edge of the new bridge he'd built across the stream before his house. He watched his son ride far down the road. Finally, where the road curved behind a mountain, the boy was lost from sight.

"Go in safety," Sir Perry whispered. His words blended with the quiet rush of the stream below. "And on the day you truly understand what you've done, my son, may you remember me well."

Slowly he moved across the bridge and back into his house. In the front hallway he was met by a servant coming from the dining room. Through the doorway behind the servant he saw the big table filled with food.

"Sir Perry," the servant said quietly, "it's noon. Shall I call everyone?"

Sir Perry grimaced, knowing at once that the saddest moments in the days ahead would be mealtimes. Always they had eaten together — he and Jules, his older son, and Erric, and the servants as well, all gathered twice a day to enjoy the abundant food and to laugh and sing

and to talk and plan. Sir Perry almost smiled to remember the astonishing amounts that could be eaten by both his sons, especially Erric, still growing as he was into manhood.

Through the doorway he could see the chair where Erric always sat — Erric, who even while eating so much could still laugh the most and talk the most as well. Strong, young Erric, who loved working and playing even more than eating. Brave, bright Erric, who so enjoyed questions and challenges and every adventure that life brought his way.

Every day in every season, Sir Perry came to the bridge, watching.

"Shall I call everyone?" the servant asked again.

But Sir Perry could not answer. He strode into the dining room, kneeled at Erric's chair, and cried.

There was much work on the farm in those days in which Sir Perry could help Jules and the servants, especially now with Erric gone. So he kept as busy as he could. But several times each day he also stood on the bridge to watch. Sometimes in the hot afternoon sun, sometimes in moonlight, sometimes in the rain and wind, he would stand and look down the empty road for Erric.

The harvest season ended, and the resting season came. Then came planting season, and growing season, and another harvest. And every day in every season, Sir Perry came to the bridge, watching.

That is where he stood late one afternoon, when as far down the road as he could see — where it came out from behind the mountain — someone appeared. The traveler wore no coat, Sir Perry noticed first, and the steps he took were weak and weary. The legs and arms were quite thin, the hair ragged, uncut. And the face —

Sir Perry strained his eyes. *The face* —

He stepped across the bridge and down the road. Then he gathered up the bottom of his robe, and began running.

Closer and closer to the traveler he ran, and his eyes soon proved what his heart already knew: His son had come home.

They met and embraced, and kept the embrace, saying nothing.

Finally Erric fell on his knees.

"Father," he cried, "Father, I was so wrong!"

Sir Perry laid his hand on Erric's head.

"I did wrong to God," Erric continued, "and I did wrong to you. I— I—"

Sir Perry lifted his son to his feet, embracing him again. Then he gripped his hands on Erric's shoulders as he looked closer at his son's frail limbs and ragged clothing.

They heard someone call, and turned to see one of the servants hurrying down the road from the house.

Sir Perry called to him: "Go back — go back at once and fetch my son a robe!"

The servant halted.

"My best robe!" Sir Perry added.

The servant nodded, and dutifully turned to go back.

Sir Perry called after him once more: "And shoes! Bring shoes!"

Looking over his shoulder, the servant nodded again.

Sir Perry took his son's slender hand, then quickly called after the servant once more: "A ring! Bring a gold ring too!"

Sir Perry smiled, and looked toward the house. "Now let's go back and get everyone working," he said. "We have a feast to prepare! And your chair at our table has been empty far too long."

He turned. But Erric didn't move.

"Father," he said, "there's more you must know."

Sir Perry stopped to listen.

"Father, I lost all your money. I've been wild and foolish. I wasted every penny and everything else I took. Nothing's left. Nothing!"

Erric took a step back, and Sir Perry watched his frown deepen.

"And I *became* nothing," Erric said.

He dropped his chin, unable to face his father's eyes. "A starving pig-feeder! That's all I was. I felt like dying."

Once more the father rushed to enclose the son in his arms.

Then he turned to walk him home. "Tonight,"

he exclaimed, "tonight my house will see the greatest celebration it's ever known! Because my son, who was dead, is now alive! My son who was lost is now here!"

Inside the house, the celebration began with more embracing, and grew steadily into feasting and singing and dancing.

The only empty chair in the dining room was that belonging to Jules. Sir Perry knew, however, that his older son would soon be back from his work in the fields.

Then a servant whispered in his ear: "Jules refuses to come in, sir. Though we've told him everything."

Sir Perry excused himself, and found Jules in the darkness, just outside a back door.

"All these years!" Jules shouted, raising an arm. "*All these years* I've worked for you, worked hard for you, never once disobeying you. And for what reward? Never once a celebration in my honor. No dances. No banquets.

"But now this spoiled, prideful, shameful son of yours comes dragging home after trashing your money and disgracing your name. And what's your discipline? *You throw a party!*"

Jules whirled on his heels to turn his back to his father.

Sir Perry pressed a hand against the stone archway beside him.

"Jules," he said, "has it meant nothing to you that we've never had to be separated? Have you forgotten that my table has always been yours, as well as everything else I own? Even this feast tonight is for your pleasure as much as anyone's."

A burst of laughter came from the merry-makers inside. Then came the startling sound of Erric's rich voice ringing out in song. It was a melody they all had sung in days long ago.

"Jules — oh, my son," Sir Perry pleaded, "don't you hear that? Your brother is alive tonight! He was as good as dead. We let him go, and lost him...

"But just listen! Erric is back. I found him! And now, Jules, he's yours to find as well."

Good Neighbor

LUKE 10:30-37

DOROTHY SLOWLY FINISHED freshening her lipstick. "Dayton," she said to her husband, "was that someone in trouble back there?"

"Back where, dear?" her husband cheerfully answered.

"Oh," she said, "up the hill a ways. I thought perhaps a car had run off the road."

"Maybe you're right," Dayton said. "I did catch something in the corner of my vision. But of course, on such a curvy highway I have to keep my eyes on the road." He stole a quick look at his wife and winked.

"Just thought I'd mention it," Dorothy said. "I know how much you love to help strangers in need. But we *are* a little late for the party. As a pastor and his wife we mustn't set a bad example by ever being tardy. You know how strongly I feel about that."

"Good reminder, dear," Dayton replied. "And it would be troublesome to turn back now, this far down the road. However, I did notice another car behind us."

He cleared his throat, and spoke reverently: "O Lord, please help that other car to stop and offer assistance."

"Oh, Dayton," Dorothy said as she powdered her nose. "How grateful I am to have married such a considerate man!"

❦

WITHOUT SLOWING his sports car, Bruce turned to look back. "Wow!" he said. "Did you see that?"

"Yeah," Brenda answered. "What a smash-up."

"Looks like it just happened," Bruce said. "I saw steam coming from the hood. We'd better call the police when we get to the party."

"Sure," Brenda agreed.

"But," said Bruce, "they'll ask questions. We'll have to tell them we didn't stop."

"So?"

"So maybe we should go back."

"Are you crazy?" Brenda said. "Look at this road. There's no place to turn around."

Bruce thought it over.

"And we've got an even better excuse," Brenda added. "You're late for a party where you're the guest of honor, because you just finished Bible college."

Bruce nodded. "Yeah. I guess the Lord's work does come first, doesn't it?"

ANGELO STOPPED HIS pickup and got out.

"*Queda!*" he said to his dog in the back. "Stay, Lobo!"

Lobo whined, but stayed put while Angelo rushed down the roadbank to where he had seen the crashed car.

He opened the car door and saw a white-haired man lying on the front seat. He reached in and touched his forehead.

The old man opened his eyes.

"I'm here to help," Angelo said calmly. "Where do you hurt most?"

The man groaned. "Oh—thank you for stopping," he said. "I'll be all right. Just shaken up."

Angelo examined him, and helped him slowly move his arms and legs.

"All in one piece, right?" the man said.

"Yeah," Angelo answered. "But let's get you out of here. I'm strong. I'll carry you."

He put his arms around him, and carefully helped him sit up. "Wait," said the man. "I'm—a little dizzy."

"Just sit a moment," Angelo said gently.

After a moment, he looked up to the truck and whistled lightly. The dog jumped out and came running to his master.

"His name is Lobo," Angelo said. "It means *wolf.*" He grinned, and gave the dog's head a hard scratch.

From a shirt pocket, Angelo pulled out his harmonica. "We'll serenade you while you rest," he said.

He played a song that started slow. When he reached a faster part, the dog began howling along.

The old man smiled. When the song was finished, Lobo climbed in the car and put a paw in the man's lap, and licked his chin.

The man laughed, and patted the dog's neck.

"Where were you headed, anyway?" Angelo asked.

"Not far from here. A place called the Oasis, down the highway. I have friends and family there. I think it's just a few miles. I could be mistaken, though—I lived around here once, but that was years ago."

"No, you're right," Angelo said. "I know the place. I'll take you. Then we'll decide what to do about your car. Ready to go?"

The old man nodded.

> *From a shirt pocket, Angelo pulled out his harmonica. "We'll serenade you while you rest."*

Angelo lifted him out, and carried him up the hill in his arms.

"By the way," he said as they traveled down the highway, "let me introduce myself. I'm Angelo, from Juarez, across the border."

"I'm Foster," said the old man. "From Minnesota." He extended his hand to shake Angelo's.

"You're far from home," Angelo said.

Foster nodded. "I've come for a special occasion — a dinner party tonight at the Oasis, in honor of my nephew. He just graduated from Bible college. The boy's pastor and his wife will be there too. When they were younger, I taught them both in Sunday school."

The bright lights of the Oasis were now in sight.

"What's more," Foster said, as Angelo turned off the highway, "none of them know I'm coming. They're going to be shocked."

Angelo grinned. "I hope it's a great surprise," he said, as he eased the truck to a stop.

A Rich Fool

LUKE 12:16-21

NTONIO SAID A QUICK PRAYER. Then he stepped through the doorway, and saw his master seated at his counting table.

He was inspecting a coin in a candle's light, the only light in the room.

"Master, you sent for me," Antonio announced.

The man looked up. The paleness of his face worried Antonio. He wondered if his master was ill.

"Young man," his master said gravely, "I have a request."

Antonio nodded. "Certainly, sir."

"Come closer," his master ordered.

"Of course, sir." Antonio stepped near. As usual, the room was crowded with accounting books, business papers, and money. His master rarely stopped working long enough to straighten anything.

His eyes glistened in the candlelight. Did Antonio see tears?

"Antonio," he said, "you've always been faithful to me, and most wise. I trust you above all others."

Antonio smiled. He had heard these words many times. His master always paused after speaking them, waiting for Antonio's response.

"Thank you, sir," he answered.

His master laid the coin on the open pages of a ledger book at his side, and gazed into the candle's flame. "Antonio... Antonio, I've been thinking very hard."

Here were words Antonio had never heard from his master's lips. He leaned forward.

"As you know," his master said, "my business has prospered magnificently this year. I earned more than I thought possible. Yes, I know I worked harder than ever, that's true. But never has my labor been so fruitful. Truly I am rich today beyond my dearest dreams. I'm surrounded by money — *and I don't know what to do with it all.*"

His eyes glistened in the candlelight. Did Antonio see tears? A spark of hope flickered in his heart. Were his prayers for his master being answered? Would he finally stop keeping all this money to himself? Would he begin caring for the poor — for the sick and needy who filled the city in these troubled times? Would he help them get better clothes and better houses and food, and Bibles and books as well? There was so much his master could do!

"Yes, loyal Antonio," his master continued, "I've been thinking deeply. And this is what I've decided: I will build my own bank. Its doors will be silver, the floors and walls will be marble, and it will have a golden roof — so beautiful it makes me cry to think of it! I'll keep all my money there. And I'll stop working. I don't need a single penny more. I'll simply enjoy

the riches I have. Day after day I'll be happy, and year after year after year.

"And this is my request, Antonio: Will you be in charge of building my bank, and storing my riches? For the rest of my years, I want no one but you to handle my money. Will you do this, wise Antonio? For me?"

Antonio could only blink. He swallowed hard. He searched his mind and heart for the right answer.

"Sir," he began. "Sir..."

"Now, now, Antonio," said his master. "Such a job is a high honor and privilege, and no doubt you feel unworthy. Yet I insist that you have it. You've always been faithful and wise, and I have no family, and I trust you above all others.

"But we'll talk more tomorrow. I don't feel well, and I have much work this evening before I rest."

His master turned to his open ledger book, and picked up the coin lying there. "Antonio, do you know why coins are flat?" he asked.

Silently, Antonio shook his head.

His master smiled. "So we can stack them, and store them, and keep them."

He picked up a pen and began his work, marking carefully in his ledger book. "Good night," he said, without looking up.

Antonio trudged to his quarters. He fell asleep that night praying for his master's soul.

A knock at his door awakened him, and a shout from another servant: "Antonio, the master has taken ill and died!"

In the darkness, Antonio shuddered.

Three days later the body was buried. Antonio wept beside his master's grave. There he knelt, and read aloud these words of Jesus:

A rich man's land yielded an abundant crop. So he asked himself, "What should I do? I've run out of room to store my crops." So he said, "I'll do this: I'll tear down my barns and build bigger ones. That's where I'll store all my produce and my possessions. And I'll tell myself, You've stored enough away to last you many years. So take it easy — eat, drink, and be merry!"

But God said to him, "You fool! This very night your life is to be taken from you. And then who will enjoy the things you have hoarded?"

That is how it will be for everyone who hoards treasure for himself but isn't rich toward God.

As for the money left behind by Antonio's master, the judges of that city met together to consider what to do. Knowing Antonio to be a godly and loyal servant of the man, they placed him in charge of all his master's riches.

From that moment on, Antonio was always bestowing money and gifts on the poor throughout the city. And he often said, "Do you know why a coin is round? So you can roll it on to someone else, and give it away."

Two Men Praying

LUKE 18:10-14

 SAW THOSE TWO MEN. But they could not see me, for I'm an angel, a messenger from heaven. And I love to come and watch God's people pray.

One man raised his hands, and said, "I thank You, God, that I'm not like other people." He touched his forehead, and nodded.

I sadly shook my head. "God will ignore such a prayer," I said, though of course he couldn't hear me.

"I'm never greedy, O God," he went on.

"I'm not unfair," he said, a little louder.

"I don't take what isn't mine!" he shouted.

He heard someone behind him. Looking over his shoulder he saw the other man. He scowled at him until the other man saw him.

Then he turned and closed his eyes again. He leaned back his head.

"Thank You, God," he announced, "that I'm not bad like that man behind me! But as You know well, I do so many good things. I'm such a very good person — as You know well."

Looking over his shoulder he saw the other man. He scowled at him until the other man saw him.

"No," I said. "You're prideful and selfish. Your heart is harder than the stone you stand on. So your words today count for nothing with God."

But of course, the man wouldn't hear me.

Behind him, the other man struck his chest with his fist. "God," he whispered, "I'm a sinner..."

"Ah, surely God hears your every word," I quickly said.

Bowing lower, he fell to his knees. "I did wrong, God," he prayed. "Have mercy on me!"

"Yes!" I cried aloud. "God's mercy endures forever! When His people confess their sins, He forgives their sins!"

The man lifted his face. His eyes sparkled with tears.

He could speak no more.

"And the man whom God forgives," I added, "can go on his way with joy."

The man stood, and walked out. All the way home I watched over him. And all the way there I whispered, "God is smiling at you now."

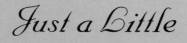Just a Little

MATTHEW 13:33, 16:6

IT WAS BAKING DAY, and I was Grandma's helper. A blueberry pie sat on the window sill to cool.

Grandma and I had just filled four baskets with fresh bread loaves. Grandma would give away most of them tomorrow after church, when she went calling on friends and neighbors.

"Who will you share the pie with?" I asked. Grandma would never keep a whole pie for just us.

"We'll think of someone," she said. "Always do."

I plopped on a kitchen stool, and gazed out the open door across Grandma's backyard. Her kitchen was still hot from the oven, but everything outside looked cool. Grandma wouldn't mind if I stepped out to play. But first I would help her clean up.

I reached for the broom beside the door. Out on the bay, I saw a sailboat that looked like the Dovers' boat. Danny Dover was probably sailing with his big brother. Tomorrow at church he would no doubt boast about how far they went, and how fast. Danny Dover could sure brag.

But he wouldn't have the most to brag about tomorrow. I was going to prove once and for all that I was smarter than him.

Grandma was putting away the baking things. "Did you know," I said to her, "that tomorrow we have a Scripture memory contest in Sunday school? Girls versus boys. I memorized ten extra verses this week just to make sure I beat Danny Dover. I can't wait to see his face when we win."

"Here," Grandma said. "Please put this in the ice-box for me." She held out a small, brown crockery pot.

"What's in it?" I asked, taking it from her.

"Yeast. For the bread." She stepped to the sink to wash her mixing bowls.

I lifted the lid and took a peek. The yellowish stuff inside smelled funny. "I don't remember putting this in," I said.

"I mixed in just a spoonful," Grandma answered, "while you measured salt and sugar. Just a little yeast works through the whole batch of dough."

I pulled down the shiny steel latch on the ice-box door, and set the yeast on the rack inside. "Yeast. What's it do?"

"Makes the bread rise," Grandma answered. "Puffs it all up."

"How does it work?"

"Don't know," Grandma said. "But it always does."

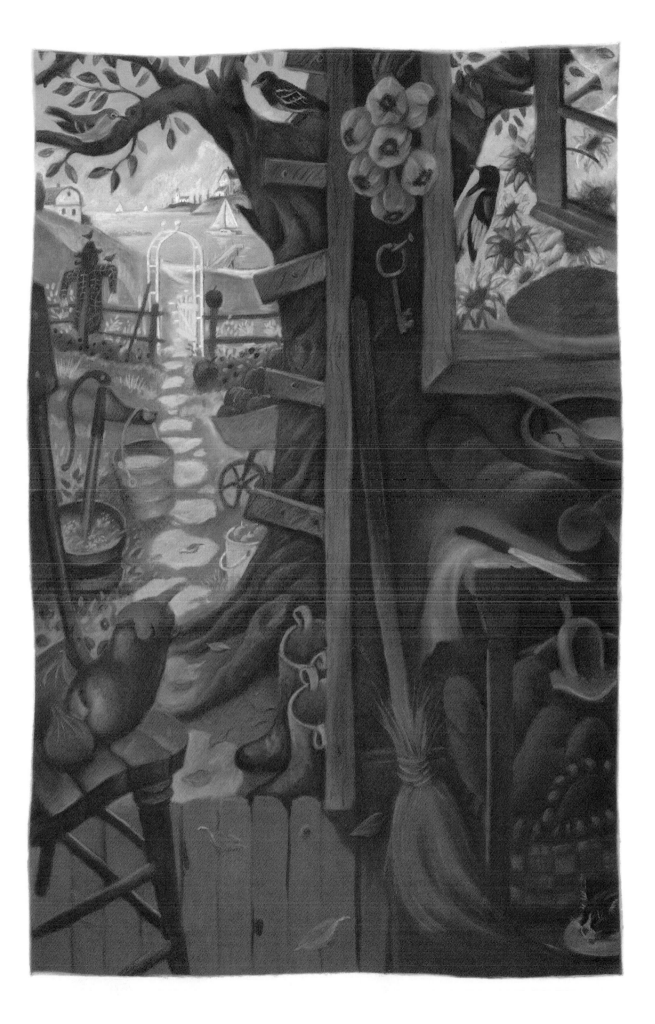

"If I ate a bite," I asked, "would it make me grow — or make me sick?"

Grandma laughed. "If it did anything," she said, "I suppose it might puff you up. But we wouldn't want that, now would we?"

I smiled, and shook my head.

"Besides," Grandma said, "Jesus said to watch out for it."

"He did?"

"Yep. 'Be on your guard against the yeast of the Pharisees.' That's what He said."

"Oh, yeah. I memorized that verse once."

"Then I'm sure you know," said Grandma, "that the Pharisees were overproud folks who liked to show off their religion. And when just a little of their ugly pride gets loose, it works its way into everything.

"I suppose," Grandma continued, "that if a Pharisee came to your class tomorrow, he could quote an awful lot of Bible verses. But he'd be puffy and stuffy and braggy about it. And the whole class might soon go sour."

"I'm glad there won't be a Pharisee there," I commented.

"I hope there won't be," Grandma said.

With dishrag in hand, she stepped to the window and looked out. "Looks like the Dovers' boat is making for shore," she noted. She turned to me. "Why don't you go meet them? Invite Danny and his brother over for blueberry pie. While they're here, tell Danny all about those new verses. You can offer to help him learn them too."

"Help him!" I exclaimed. "But what about the contest?"

"Hurry along now," Grandma said, nudging me to the door. "Before you miss those boys. I'll finish cleaning."

Grandma's insistence got me out the door and across the backyard. But at the gate I stopped. I couldn't take another step. I stood there, staring at the Dovers' boat nearing shore.

I felt Grandma's warm hands on my shoulders. "You know, Sugar," she said, "the happiness you'll get from beating Danny won't last any longer than one of my blueberry pies around here. But if you forget this bragging business — just think how pleased you'll be if you can help Danny instead, and maybe end up helping the whole class too. Now there's a good feeling that will last forever!

"But," she said, "I'll let you decide." She lifted her hands from my shoulders.

Down at the shore, I saw the boys bringing down the sails.

I turned and faced Grandma. "That pie will taste much better while it's warm, won't it?"

"Always does," she answered.

I gave her a quick kiss. "Then I'll run and get the Dover boys." I dashed out the gate, thinking about which new verse to share first with Danny.

Pearl Beyond Price

MATTHEW 13:45-46

SARAH PEARLY WAS TURNING OUT the last lamp in the bookshop when she heard tapping at the window.

Seeing a man outside, she left the lamp on. She hurried to a back doorway. "Father!" she called.

Her father stepped from the back. He had just put on his coat. When he saw the well-dressed man at the window, he stepped quickly across the little shop to unlock the front door.

"What is it, sir?" he said as he swung the door open.

The man stood still before the window, staring down. "That — that ball of beauty!" he said.

"What?" said her father.

Understanding at once, Sarah stepped closer. On the wide window sill, a snowy pearl the size of a marble lay on the open pages of her grandfather's old Bible, with other books displayed nearby. Through all the years in which her father had struggled to keep the bookshop open, he had kept the pearl in his front window — just for show, he said, to help people remember his name and his shop.

He turned to his daughter. She gazed into his eyes. "It's okay, Father," she whispered.

The pearl was so unusual in size and color that his customers thought it was fake. Even her father once told Sarah he didn't think it was real. "Even if it is," he said, "it seems too big and strange to be worn as jewelry. And a pearl has no value except to wear."

"I think it's beautiful just where it is," Sarah had answered.

Smiling, her father promised to give her both the pearl and the Bible on her twelfth birthday. And now that was only a day away.

Her father spoke to the well-dressed man again. "What did you say, sir?"

The man kept staring through the window. "Splendid as the moon," he said. "And nearly as big. An utterly unbelievable pearl!"

Sarah's father examined the man's face, then looked down at the pearl.

"I'm glad you like it, sir. Just a little ornamentation for a humble shop. Now if you can excuse us please, we must close for the evening." He stepped back inside.

The man rushed to the doorway. "Wait! Please! This pearl — where on earth did it come from?"

"I don't know," said her father. "Maybe from an oyster."

"Please," said the man, "don't joke with me. Besides, it doesn't matter where it came from. All that matters is that I have it. You see, I'm a trader of fine jewels. I've traveled the world, been in a hundred seaports, shopped a thousand shops. I *know* pearls. And I'm persuaded there is none like this in all the world. Yes, I must have it."

"But this is a bookshop, sir," her father said. "The pearl isn't even for sale."

"Simply name the price," the man said. "I am L. J. Vanson of Vanson Jewelers, Limited, in London." He pulled a card from his pocket. Sarah's father carefully read it.

"I see," he said quietly.

He turned to his daughter. She gazed into his eyes. "It's okay, Father," she whispered.

He turned back to the man standing in the doorway, and took a deep breath. "I'm afraid it's beyond your price, sir."

The man's eyes grew large. "Please, please understand!" he exclaimed. "The price matters nothing. I can afford thousands. I can afford tens of thousands. Many tens of thousands!"

Sarah watched her father's face. He seemed stunned. He looked down at the floor. Was he calculating a price? Or thinking about her birthday? What could she say if he turned to her again? She decided to mention that they would still have the old Bible — and didn't that mean more than any pearl?

Finally her father looked up. "Mr. Van-

son," he said, "I cannot and will not sell the pearl, and I ask that you say nothing more about it. Good evening, Mr. Vanson." He began pushing the door closed.

Mr. Vanson's eyes were piercing, and he seemed immovable. But as the door came slowly toward him, he stepped stiffly back into the street, tipped his hat to them both, and walked away.

Sarah stepped near her father as he leaned over the window sill. He picked up the pearl and rolled it in his hand. Then he read aloud the verses circled on the open page of the old Bible:

The kingdom of heaven is like a merchant seeking beautiful pearls. When he found one pearl of extremely high value, he sold all he owned and bought it.

Her father looked out the window. "It doesn't make sense, Sarah," he said. "I don't understand why a man would give up so much money—for a pearl!"

"But Father!" Sarah said. "Didn't you just do exactly that?"

He turned to her, and winked. "I guess there's quite a lot in life worth more than money," he said. "All the money in the world."

He took her hand, and wrapped her fingers around the pearl. "Happy Birthday," he said. Then he reached for the old Bible, closed it, and placed it under her arm.

"Thank you," she whispered.

They walked away from the window, and her father turned out the lamp. They made their way through the darkened shop for the back door, and for home.

Hidden Treasure

MATTHEW 13:44

AFTER LIFTING OUT the treasure chest and unlatching it, Nicholas Himmel threw his feathered cap in the air, and leaped. "Sing with me, birds!" he shouted. "Rejoice with me, breeze! Dance with me, flowers!"

"What's that commotion?" growled old Doctor Griff as he hurried from his house below. Coming closer, he stood in silent amazement at what he saw: sunlight sparkling on pearls and diamonds, on emeralds and rubies, and on gold and silver.

A smile slowly pushed aside his frown. "May God be praised!" he finally said. "You found it!"

"I did!" Nicholas replied. He jumped and clicked his heels. He even turned a cartwheel.

Doctor Griff calmed him down enough to shake his hand. "Nicholas," he said, "I gave you my word—and I'll stick to it."

"And by sundown," answered Nicholas, "I'll be at your house with the payment."

That evening, at dinner with his family, Nicholas kept repeating his account of the day's happenings.

"So," his wife Hilda asked again, "you went to the bank and took out *all* our savings?"

"Yes," Nicholas answered.

"And paid it *all* to Doctor Griff—for that land?"

"Yes."

"It's more than the land is worth," Hilda said.

"But it was our agreement long ago," Nicholas declared. "If I ever found the old treasure on his land — the lost prince's treasure that's been rumored for centuries to be there somewhere — then Doctor Griff agreed to secretly sell me the property for eighty spitzmarks. And he's as good as his word, God bless him. Now the land is ours — and the treasure too."

Hilda closed her eyes and drummed her forehead with her fingers. "But — but you *buried* the treasure again?"

"Yes, my lovely Hilda, and don't worry: I'll still be making and selling the finest watches and clocks in the valley. Watchmakers are always in demand — till the end of *time!*" He chuckled at his favorite joke.

Franz, the older of his two sons, rested his elbows on the table. "Truly, Father — you hid the treasure again?"

"And very well, too!" Nicholas answered, raising one eyebrow.

> *Hilda closed her eyes and drummed her forehead with her fingers. "But — but you buried the treasure again?"*

"But why, Father?" asked Gustav, the younger boy.

"Ha! I thought you'd never ask! I hid it so my sons — if they want to — can know the joy of seeking and finding that treasure for themselves!"

"Really?" both boys exclaimed.

"YES!" Nicholas clapped his hands. "My joy isn't real joy until I share it. But before you search, there's a couple of things we have to do. In the meantime..." He reached into his pocket and pulled out four fifty-mark gold pieces. "This should replenish our savings."

"Nicholas!" shouted Hilda. "Will you never stop surprising me?"

"Never," her husband answered.

Some time later, the four Himmels were seated under a tree on their new land, enjoying a new morning. Lying beside them were shovels and picks. Nicholas bent over and smelled the wildflowers waving in the wind. "I love how you're dressed this morning," he told them. "Not even kings and queens have finer robes than you."

Far above, skylarks were flying and chirping. Nicholas called out to them, "Always singing, eh? Yes, and I know why! Because you understand that God in heaven takes care of you."

From far below they heard the chimes in the village clocktower. Then they saw Doctor Griff walking up the hill to them, carrying his Bible.

He greeted them and sat down. Nicholas turned to his family, took off his cap, and quoted this parable:

> *The kingdom of heaven is like treasure buried in a field, which a man found and then hid again. In his joy he sells everything he has and buys that field.*

"To prepare our family for this day," Nicholas continued, "I asked that we all do two things: First, decide how to spend the treasure, if Franz and Gustav can find it. And second, figure out what this parable of Jesus means.

"We've done the first thing. We've decided to give most of the treasure away, once it's dug up again. We'll give generously to all the churches in this valley, and to every person here who is poor and in need.

"And now: What could the parable mean? We aren't sure. That's why I asked Doctor Griff for help. Doctor, what do you say?"

"I say what I always say," replied the old doctor: "The best stories are the stories with the best heroes. And this little story has the best Hero of all."

"Who's that?" young Gustav asked.

"Close your eyes, all of you," said the doctor, "and listen for clues."

All the Himmels closed their eyes.

"The story," Doctor Griff said in his gravelly voice, "is about a field. Now Jesus Himself tells us, in this same Bible chapter, that 'the field is the world.'

"And in this field, so the story goes, there's treasure. Does this world have treasure? Of course it does! God made this world, and God never makes junk. Everything in this world was made to give Him praise and glory. He wants a world where people shine with brightness — yes, there's the real treasure: all that brightness and glory to God.

"But, the story says, this treasure is buried. Where is the world's bright glory buried? It's buried deep under the darkness of sin.

"And now, the story tells us, a certain man found this treasure. Who could that be? Only one Man could lift off that heavy darkness, and bring back the brightness. And that's exactly why He came to this world. Just by coming here, and being here, and living His life, He uncovered the treasure. He showed us how bright and good a man can really be.

"He wanted to share this glory with us. But it wasn't His plan to do it all at once. No, after showing us, He decided to keep the brightness hidden a while. Still, He told us secret stories about it — like this story — stories that only His people can truly understand.

"Then this Man had a job to do. It was terrible work, awful work. But He did it without complaining. In fact, the Bible says He did it for the *joy* set before Him.

"And what was that work? The story tells us: He had to sell everything He owned. He had to give up everything. He had to empty Himself. He was full of life, and full of God, but He had to lose all that. Yes — He had to die.

"Sad, isn't it? But don't despair! What does the story say? After selling everything, this Man *bought that field.* The field, the world, belongs to Him now. It's all His property. Someday — when the time is right — this Man will come back here, and we'll see Him as glorious as He can be. He'll share His brightness with His people. We'll shine like treasure in the sunlight.

"So now you know the Hero," Doctor Griff concluded. "All of you, say His name out loud."

They all answered, *"Jesus."*

"Yes, my friends. That's what the parable means to me. Now if you think this old doctor may be right, then for heaven's sake follow Jesus' example, and get His bright treasure, no matter what it costs you."

The chimes in the clocktower rang again.

"Time to start searching," Nicholas said to his sons. He stood, and handed them shovels. "And whenever you boys get close to the treasure," he added, "I'll let you know by turning a few cartwheels."

After the Storm

MATTHEW 7:24-27

ARLY ON THE MORNING after the hurricane, Luke and Lucy Stone looked out the back of their home on Judgment Island. The first thing they saw was the wreckage of the new house belonging to their neighbors, Mike and Marcy Merryweather.

It had been a cute cottage, with a kitchen built like a lighthouse. But now the pounding waves had washed over and through it all, leaving the place in ruins. The Merry-weathers stood nearby.

"Mike! Marcy!" Luke called. "You can stay with us now."

"Yes," said Lucy. "Come have breakfast!"

"Forget it," Marcy called back, as she and Mike stepped down through the sand toward the wreckage. "We'll just clean everything up, and be back to normal in no time."

"After all," said Mike, "the foundation is as sturdy and stable as ever."

"But Mike!" protested Luke. "The storm washed all the sand out from under you. When the tide comes in, what's left of your house will only wash away. Forget that place!"

"I'm not sure I trust your advice," Mike answered. "When I built this house, you kept insisting it would crash into the sea in the first storm. I insisted it wouldn't. Well, Luke, the big storm has come and gone—and our place is still standing, isn't it? So there. You were wrong, I was right." He headed through the lighthouse door.

"Don't be foolish!" Luke shouted. "Get away before the tower goes over!"

Lucy pleaded: "Listen to us, please!"

"Oh, we don't mind listening," Marcy answered. "Just don't expect us to do anything about it." She stepped into the tower behind her husband.

Suddenly a giant wave came breaking on the shore. It crashed into the cottage and rushed around the lighthouse. That was all it took. The tower creaked and jerked, then tumbled into the foam and slid out to deeper water. Lucy screamed to see it, and she and Luke came running to the water's edge.

That was all it took. The tower creaked and jerked, then tumbled into the foam and slid out to deeper water.

A moment later, Mike and Marcy appeared, floating out of the tower's broken base. They were riding on their kitchen table. Mike was paddling with a broken plank. Marcy was whistling.

Luke yelled: "Don't worry—we'll get the boat and come after you!"

"Don't bother," Mike called back. "We're leaving."

"For a good sandy spot somewhere else," Marcy added. "We're going to rebuild!"

Luke and Lucy watched them disappear around the edge of the island. They never saw the Merryweathers again.

They walked back into their own house, which was built on rock. They enjoyed a breakfast of fried fish and biscuits and rice pudding and cranberry juice. Then, as they did every morning, they sat down by the front window to study their Bibles together, and listen carefully for God to tell them what to do.